How to Care for Your Pet Rabbit

Including Choosing the Best Breeds for Pets

By Amber Richards

Table Of Contents

Introduction

This is a good resource for pet owners, and those considering getting a rabbit as a pet. Because the focus of this book is for pet owners (and future rabbit owners) to learn how to provide a great home for their pet, I have intentionally not covered the topic of breeding rabbits in this book. That is a complex subject for a book of it's own, and most pet owners do not breed their rabbits.

A pet rabbit can be housed indoors or out and this book shows you both methods, so you can decide which is best for your situation.

Amber Richards

Why Rabbits?

I had a rabbit as a child that I loved dearly. He was a black, medium sized rabbit I named Midnight, whom we found hiding under our home that we adopted (as we couldn't find his owners). I remember bringing him into our home and he played with our huge German Shepard dog and Manx cat famously. They would chase each other (including the rabbit chasing the dog and cat), and he would actually snuggle and sleep with them at times.

Whenever guests came to our home, they nearly always wanted me to bring him inside to watch him play with the other animals and to enjoy his company. He lived outdoors mainly, but was regularly brought indoors for play time. He was a very popular, well liked pet around our neighborhood, and brought much joy to many.

When I was an adult, I decided to get my children into 4H with a rabbit. Long story short, they lost interest and mine grew! I then discovered the little niche of adult rabbit breeders and rabbit shows and was hooked. I raised Mini rex rabbits for several years and took some wins with my rabbits at national level competitions. The breeds listed in this book are recognized breeds from the American Rabbit Association (ARBA in America), although there are other breeds out there as well. I have also judged a county fair 4H rabbit show and helped many 4H children with their rabbits.

If you already own a rabbit, or are not searching for a particular breed for a pet, you might want to skip over the sections about breeds, for it is extensive. It is meant to be an aid for those who have not yet obtained a rabbit and wish to research the various breeds available.

I write this book out of a great love for these animals, and a desire to share my experiences so others can discover the joy of owning a pet rabbit. Over the years, they have brought so many fond moments and created memories for me that I'll always cherish.

With pet ownership, of course, comes responsibility in knowing how to give them a proper home and care, so they are healthy and happy.

Rabbits are said to have originated in the western Mediterranean. They were introduced to Britain by the Normans and were valued for their fur as well as meat. It is believed that domesticated breeding began in the Middle Ages. In the 18th century, there were a variety of different types. By the 19th century, breeding rabbits for exhibiting in the U S was becoming popular and by the Victorian era, they were being kept as household pets.

During this period one of the first imported breeds was the Belgian Hare. This was in 1888 and soon after the American Belgian Hare Association was formed. Although many were imported from 1898 to 1901, today this breed is considered one of the rarest, according to the American Livestock Breed Conservancy.

Rabbits as Pets

Have you decided that you would like to have a pet rabbit, or maybe you already have one and would like to learn how to care for it? Perhaps you are interested in showing rabbits like in 4H or the American Rabbit Breeders Association shows. Some also raise rabbits for their fur, especially the angoras for spinning their wool. Before you decide on which breed of rabbit you want, you will want to consider a few things. Since there are so many different breeds out there, knowing a little about each one will help you decide which one will be the best choice for your situation.

Rabbits, like many other types of pets, are very affectionate and do bond with their humans. They may not show it in the same way, but once you get used to their habits, you will know when they want attention.

Rabbits are quiet animals for the most part, but not 100% silent as many believe. They do make a grunting noise on occasion and a sound that is similar to growling. They usually only make noise when they are very scared or if they get hurt. They can scream loudly at this point (and it can be frightening to hear as well), regardless of the breed.

There are many different breeds of rabbits and they vary in size. They generally live from 7 to 9 years. The next thing you might be wondering about is if it makes a difference whether you choose a male rabbit or a female rabbit. Although most people will tell you that it is not an important aspect when choosing a rabbit for a pet, others say a male is a better choice in a general sense.

One of the things that cannot be emphasized enough is that no two rabbits, regardless of breed, sex or other factor will be identical. Some people have had rabbits that were almost like a member of the family and others have had the same breed and found that it was not a good fit as a pet for their situation.

Rabbits can be the most easy going, laid back pet you ever had or they can be a terror (and yes, some rabbits can have a nasty mean streak, a rabbit bite is bad, remember they can chew wood). They have very sharp nails as well.   Please don't let that caution scare you off towards a rabbit, its just a caution you should be aware of. Even in those cases, sometimes the rabbit can come out of that tendency. I'll share more about what to try in the later chapter of General Care in this book.

Rabbits can be very sweet, loving and affectionate pets, and this is more likely the case. In fact many will give rabbit kisses, which is licking your hand or arm, a supreme form of affection a bunny can give. I have found that most have a wonderful bond with their human (provided they are given a loving home of course), and time is spent with them.

The next section of this book, *Breeds of Rabbits*, will go into more detail on which ones seem to be the most desirable as pets. One thing you will need to think about is the male rabbit can act similar to male cats. Male cats that have not been neutered spray urine and mark their territory and male rabbits sometimes to do this as well. It is impossible to be able to tell which ones will do this and which ones will not. The incidence of it happening seems to be greatly reduced if there is not a female rabbit around.

If you have your heart set on a female rabbit, there are some disadvantages to this as well. Some do display moody symptoms revolving around their reproductive cycle.

Remember, if you have a male and a female rabbit together, you most likely will have baby rabbits, and it is true that they reproduce quite rapidly. They have even been known to be able to breed through a wire cage separating them. If they are taken out to play, it only takes a couple of seconds literally for mating to occur, and they will be more interested in that, than playing with their humans.

Plan on one cage per rabbit. Rabbits are territorial and two living together will fight. The two exceptions where it might work is two sisters obtained while they are young and have always lived together, and a pair (2 males or a male/female pair) if they have been neutered and/or spayed. Personally, I would recommend anyone wanting a pet rabbit to stick with just one, yet plan to really spend time with it, as they are social and need quality time with their humans.

Breeds of Rabbits

Breeds consist of small, medium and large. They are really cute and it is easy to fall in love with the little guys and think what a great pet they would make. You need to keep in mind, that cute does not a personality make and in the rabbit world, there are as many personalities as there are in the human world. The following are some of the types of rabbits that you might want to consider beginning with the small breeds of rabbits. Generally the ones you have to be the most cautious of for temperament is the small breeds.

Small Breeds

Britannia Petite – This breed weighs less than 2 ½ pounds and have silky coats. They are either black, black otter, ruby-eyed white or chestnut agouti. This breed is somewhat excitable and jittery and is generally not the best choice for a pet. They are also fine boned and delicate.

Dutch – Weighing from 3 ½ to 5 ½ pounds, the Dutch rabbit has a white body with black, chocolate, tortoise, blue or brown or steel colors. The face is all white as are the back feet. They are a great choice for a pet because they are calm and get along well with children. Dutch rabbits have a unique pattern of color that is unique to this breed alone.

Dwarf Hotot – The Dwarf Hotot (pronouned Ho Toe) is a smaller version of a larger breed. This one weighs under 3 pounds and has a white body with black rings around the eyes, almost looking like they have makeup on. Some say they have a good personality and others say they do not. Choose this breed with care.

Havana – A little larger than the previous rabbits, the Havana weighs from 4 ½ pounds to 6 ½ pounds. They are a good choice if you are looking for a pet bunny.

They generally come is solid colors, black, blue &

chocolate (brown) and are known for their very shiny,

glossy fur.

Himalayan – This small breed of rabbit has a long,

slender body and is like the dachshund of rabbits. The

body is white and points (nose, ears, tail & feet) are

either lilac, chocolate, blue or black. They generally

weigh from 2 ½ pounds to 4 ½ pounds. This breed

makes an excellent pet as they are known for their

gentle disposition.

Lionhead – This breed is the newest addition of breeds accepted into the ARBA (at the time of this writing), the varieties officially accepted are Tortoise and Ruby-eyed white. Weighing between 2 ½ to 3 ¾ pounds, the Lionhead is so named for the fur that circles the head looks like a lion's mane. They have short ears – only 2 or 3 inches long – and most owners say they are friendly and great to have as pets. They are smart and some people have trained them to obey commands, such as come, eat and play.

Mini Satin – This breed is new to the American Rabbit Breeders Association (ARBA) and has fur much like the larger breed Satin. Weighing from 3 ¼ pounds to 4 ¾ pounds, they are well liked because of their satiny fur and their gentle disposition.

Netherland Dwarf – This breed is one of the smallest of rabbits with the cute factor off the scale! They weigh less than 2 ½ pounds. Their head is more round than most breeds and their ears are shorter. Available in a variety of colors. This is one breed that is very popular in the pet market, but caution should be heeded. Many in this breed are down right mean.

Polish – A round body and short ears are two of the traits of the Polish bunny. They weigh under 3 ½ pounds and colors include ruby-eyed white, blue-eyed white, blue, chocolate and black. Some people have not had a problem with this breed and others say they are very temperamental.

Medium Breeds

Unless stated otherwise in the description of the breeds below, the medium breeds are a good choice for a pet.

American Sable – This medium size breed weighs from 7 to 10 pounds and are quite active. They are a sepia brown and their fur is soft except for the guard hairs, which are coarse. This breed has a good disposition.

Belgian Hare – Colored a chestnut or red tan covering the blue undercoat, the Belgian Hare weighs from 6 to 9 ½ pounds. This breed is active and fun when chosen as pets. They have a unique look to them in general body shape.

Chinchilla – They have the chinchilla coloring and at 5 ½ to 6 ½ pounds are smaller than the American Chinchilla. They have good temperaments.

English Spot – Marked with a butterfly shape on the nose, a herringbone on the spine, eye rings, colored ears and spots on the body and on the cheeks, it is no wonder this breed is called English Spot. Colors include tortoise, lilac, gray, gold, chocolate, blue or black on white, this breed has a body that is similar to the shape of the Belgian Hare.

Florida White – Weighing from 4 to 6 pounds, this breed is all white with a rounded body. They are good pets.

Harlequin – A variety of colors including lilac, chocolate, blue and black are typical of the Harlequin rabbit. The color combinations are most interesting because they will alternate between white and color and often one side of their face is white with a colored ear and the other side is colored with a white ear.

Lilac – Blue gray or lilac as it is called in the bunny world, this breed weighs from 5 ½ to 8 pounds and has dense fur.
Nice personalities they have.

Rhinelander – A breed that has a white body and golden orange and black markings on each side of the rear part of their body, the Rhinelander generally weighs between 6 ½ to 10 pounds. Their nose has a butterfly mark and the ears are colored. They have circles around the eyes and spots on the cheeks.

Satin – A larger version of the Mini Satin, this breed weighs 8 ½ to 11 pounds. Included colors are chocolate, red copper, white, blue, black, Siamese, chinchilla broken group and Californian. They have very soft, shiny fur.

Silver – A fawn, brown or black fur with silver or white guard hairs, this breed weigh between 4 and 7 pounds.

Silver Marten – The Silver Marten is marked in an pattern unique to the breed with sable, chocolate, blue, or black silver-tipped guard hairs. They typically weigh between 5 and 7 ½ pounds. They are very striking.

Standard Chinchilla – This is a totally different breed than the American Chinchilla. They have the classic chinchilla coloring and weigh from 5 to 7 ½ pounds.

Tan – The Tan breed has tan on the tail, belly, chest, toes, the back of the legs, ears, jowls, nostrils and circles around the eyes. They are either lilac, chocolate, blue or black and weigh from 4 to 6 pounds. This is one of the medium breeds of rabbits that do not always have the personality needed to be a good pet.

Thrianta – This is a breed recently accepted by the ARBA and is also known as the "Fire of the Fancy". They weigh about 6 pounds and have very noticeable red-orange fur. They also have brown eyes, which set them apart from other breeds.

Large Breeds

In general the large breeds are known to have nice dispositions. It can be quite surprising how large some of these rabbits can actually get.

American – A breed that weighs from 9 to 12 pounds, American rabbits are usually gray and white. They are of medium build and have a narrow head.

American Chinchilla – Weighing 9 to 12 pounds, this breed will always have the classic chinchilla coloring. This is a black, white and gray pattern that stands out and the fur is very fine and shiny. The body of the American Chinchilla is a round shape.

American Sable – This breed can weigh as much as 10 pounds. It has distinct coloring and the eyes glow ruby red.

Beverens – The Beverens breed is from Europe and they are not common in the U.S. These rabbits can weigh as much as 12 pounds and include the colors of blue eyed whites, black and blue.

Blanc de Hotot – Pure white rabbits with black rings around the eyes, they almost look as if they are wearing eyeliner. These rabbits can weigh up to 11 pounds.

Californian – This is a breed that also has a solid white body combined with a black tail, feet, ears and nose. Their body is round and they are of medium build, weighing from 8 to 12 pounds. They have the same color pattern as the long bodies Himalyan.

Champagne d'Argent – A chubby rabbit, weighing from 9 to 12 pounds, the babies are black when they are born, but they change color around the age of 2 months. The unmistakable color is a bluish white mixed with black hairs and the under color is a slate blue.

Checkered Giant – Marked with a pattern that is unique to the Checkered Giant, this rabbit is usually all white with a butterfly mark on its nose, eye rings, spots on the body and cheeks, blue or black markings along the spine and colored ears. This is one of the large breeds that might not have the personality for a good pet.

Cinnamon – The name comes from the color, which is a cinnamon or rust with gray on the rabbit's belly and gray ticking on its back. A butterfly mark is featured on the nose and it has rings around the eyes. The inside of the hind legs has rust colored spots. This breed weighs from 5 to 11 pounds.

***Crème d'Argent* –** A breed that weighs between 8 and 11 pounds, the rabbits are a creamy white and they have an orange undercoat. They also have a butterfly marking on their nose.

***Giant Chinchilla* –** This is one of the biggest of the large breed rabbits. They weigh from 12 to 16 pounds and have the typical chinchilla coloring.

***New Zealand Whites* –** This breed is almost totally white and has pink eyes. They are also a large breed and weigh from 9 to 12 pounds. They have a very good temperament, which makes this a great choice for pets and they are also raised for their meat.

Flemish Giant (Patagonian) – This breed is the largest

of all. They are often called "Gentle Giants" because they

can weigh 13 pounds or more. The colors include white,

steely gray, sand, light gray, fawn, blue or black They

have huge tails and a long body as well as being chunky.

I have seen them on pet harnesses walking with their

humans before, although great care needs to be given

that an unknown dog doesn't approach. They are quite

fascinating to see!

Palomino – Golden and lynx in color, this breed weighs

no more than 9 ½ pounds.

Silver Fox – Weighing from 9 to 12 pounds, the Silver

Fox breed is a jet black with silver markings.

Lop Rabbit Breeds

Lop bunnies are some of the cutest breeds. Some people are only interested in the lops. This is especially true when their ears, which are supposed to hang down rather than stand up, stick straight out from their head. This is a breed that many people do not know a lot about, so the following list will help you to distinguish between the different types of lop bunnies. In general lop bunnies are fairly calm and have good personalities, making good pets.

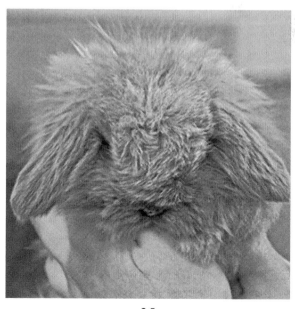

American Fuzzy Lop – This breed includes several different colors and they only weigh from 3 ½ to 4 pounds. Their fur is long and fluffy; when they are babies it can get tangled very easily and takes more care until their adult coat comes in. As they get older, it becomes easier to take care of although the rabbit will still need to be groomed, which entails brushing a couple of times weekly. The American Fuzzy Lop rabbits, along with the Holland Lops are the smallest of the breed. They are mellow rabbits and have a great temperament.

English Lops – The English Lop is a bigger rabbit, typically weighing 9 pounds or more. They also come in a number of colors and are fairly rare. They have very long ears that usually drag the floor. This is a very gentle breed and they have a great personality. In cold winter months, special care needs to be given to the ears, so they don't freeze. Usually putting a pair of socks on the ears, and gently tying the ears together on the back with a soft hair scrunchy gives protection during the coldest parts of winter. It's important to ensure their ears don't get wet. Also important is to keep an eye out for any signs of frost bite to their ears, which they can be prone to. It would be a good idea to have them housed in a garage or other enclosed building during the winter months, if at all possible. These are amazing rabbits to see!

French Lop – Another large breed, the French Lop

weighs 10 pounds and often more. There are a variety of

colors to choose from and have a muscular build. This is

a good breed for a pet because they are known to be

sweet and quite gentle. People are usually surprised at

how large they are.

Torte Holland Lop Standing Up

Holland Lop – As mentioned earlier, this breed along with the American Fuzzy Lop is one of the smallest lop breeds, weighing under 4 pounds. They come in many colors and make good pets due to their gentle nature. Commonly when people think of a lop eared bunny, this is the breed they have envisioned. They are a very popular rabbit breed, with good reason.

Mini Lop – When it comes to the lop breeds, many folks assume the Mini Lop is the smallest breed; however, it is not. This breed generally weighs from 4 ½ to 6 ½ pounds and come in many colors. They have a general reputation of not possessing the best personalities among the lop breeds. This is of course, a very generalization and many make awesome pets.

Cute baby.

Fur Breeds

The fur breeds are rabbits that are known for the quality of their fur. They include several breeds known for their silky, smooth fur that is short (the short haired ones do not need grooming) as well as the long haired breeds. Some of these should be groomed regularly because they can develop problems such as matting, hairballs and even skin decay in the worse-case scenarios, if they are neglected. This time commitment for grooming should be a consideration when deciding to choose one of the long-haired fur breeds for a pet. Take a look at some of the fur breeds below.

American Fuzzy Lop – This breed can actually be classified in either the fur breed or the lop breeds. You can read more about these rabbits in the section above on lop breeds. Adult fur care is quite easy, but the babies' fur tangles more. Great dispositions.

English Angoras – A giant ball of fur, the English

Angora generally weighs no more than 7 ½ pounds. Due

to having so much hair they look much bigger than they

are – often you cannot see their eyes! They are a gentle

breed rabbit and make good pets if you are willing to

groom. These are popular for their wool being spun into

yarn. They are quite interesting to look at as well.

French Angora – This is a bigger breed weighing from 7 ½ to 10 pounds. They do not have as much fur as the other Angora breeds. The longest fur is on the rear legs. This is another breed that is desirable if you are looking for a pet rabbit because they have a good personality.

Giant Angora – The Giant Angora is the largest among the four Angora breeds recognized by the ARBA. They are mainly white with ruby eyes. They are known for their fur, which is popular for spinning into yarn and other wool items. It is extremely soft, and an expensive yarn. They produce more than the English, Satin or French Angora and it needs to be harvested (shaved) every 90 days at the least. I've witnessed people seeing one for the first time in real life, not know what kind of animal it was, many thinking it was a type of dog.

Satin Angora – A smaller rabbit, weighing only 3 to 4 pounds, this breed is a good choice for a pet due to the gentle nature. They have very soft fur, which is easy to take care of and when used for spinning, is stronger than other types of Angora.

Jersey Woolly – This is a breed that weighs less than 3 ½ pounds and is known for their fluffy fur. They come in several different colors and the cute factor is off-the-scale. However, this can be misleading because some have less than desirable personalities. Use caution with this breed for a pet.

Mini Rex – I'll admit it, these are probably my favorite, and the breed I raised for show. A short, very densely furred rabbit, their coat feels velvety soft. They and the standard rex are the live "velveteen" rabbits. To touch them is amazing! They generally weigh between 3 and 4 ½ pounds. Colors vary and include white (ruby eyed and blue eyed), seal tortoise, red, opal, lynx, lilac, Himalayan, chocolate, chinchilla, castor, broken group, blue and black. For the most part, this breed has great personalities and make wonderful pets. As with all rabbits, it is possible to get one that is a bit temperamental.

Standard Rex – The Standard Rex breed is larger than the other mentioned previously. They usually weigh between 7 ½ and 10 ½ pounds. They come in many of the same colors – black, broken group, blue, black otter, castor, Californian, chinchilla, chocolate, lynx, lilac, red, opal, sable, white and seal. They also have the velvety fur like the Mini Rex. In addition, they are a gentle breed that is suitable as a pet.

General Care of Your Pet Rabbit

Six weeks is the earliest a baby bunny should be weaned from it's mother, with 8-9 weeks being preferable. You'll want to make sure children are calm and quiet when playing with the rabbit, as they are easily frightened, especially when getting used to a new home and people. They are also fragile and could be hurt easily.

The first few days home attention should be given frequently, but in short, quiet visits. It is recommended to have the child sit quietly on the floor with a towel on the child's lap, and the adult carefully place the rabbit on the towel. That way the child can pet the bunny without getting scratched, and there will be no worries about accidently dropping the rabbit. The rabbit will feel more secure this way as well. Alternatively, one could also place the rabbit on the floor right next to the child, always with adult supervision.

Reserve the picking up and holding bunny until both are adjusted more. When the time comes for that, prepare the child that rabbits have toenails and it is possible to get a scratch.

When a rabbit thumps loudly, it means like are in alert mode and that they are sensing danger. Do your best to reassure your pet, and make sure the rabbit is safe when this happens. It may be another animal is nearby, or kids are being too loud. They may also be seeing a predator of some sort, an eagle, owl, snake etc. Try to ascertain why he is sensing danger.

Feeding

You'll want to feed as the mainstay in your rabbit's diet a good, commercial rabbit food pellet. Usually the best and most economical place to buy the food is at a local farm store. Rabbits can be free fed, meaning their feed dish is always full, but there are some real advantages to feeding a daily portion every evening or morning. Read the manufacturer's directions for the recommended amount for the rabbit's size and breed.

If you get a baby bunny, try to obtain the exact feed the baby was on. Ideally, if you could find the exact brand and type, just keep him on that. Many breeders will give you a bag of the pellets he's been on. If you can get it, mix it 50/50 with the rabbit feed you plan on using, so there's a more gradual change to the new food. Whatever you settle on feeding in regards to a rabbit pellet, try to stick with the same brand and type throughout the rabbit's life. Don't jump around with different kinds everytime you need a new bag.

Rabbits are delicate animals and if something begins to ail their health, they tend to go downhill very fast. Not eating their daily portion of food is one of the earliest alerts that something may be wrong. This is the main benefit of feeding a daily portion, which will alert you quickly if they are not eating, otherwise known as going 'off-feed'.

Contrary to popular belief, not all rabbits eat, or even like carrots. If yours does, it's fine to give ½ a carrot a day, or a few slices of apples. Do not give rabbits lettuce, cabbage or green leafy vegetables, because it can cause diarrhea, which could lead to serious health problems for rabbits. Yes, some green vegetables may be fine (dandelion greens are great), but others are not, so to be on the safe side, avoid them altogether.

If you notice a rabbit, especially a young one, get sudden diarrhea, get the rabbit to a vet asap. This can be fatal and can kill them quickly, the only hope being early intervention. Keep a baby just on rabbit pellets and grass hay, wait for the introduction of other foods until he has reached adulthood. Their digestive systems are very sensitive.

Rabbits also benefit greatly with plenty of grass hay daily, but ensure that the hay is clean, dry and doesn't have any mold or pesticides in it. This is especially critical when they are molting their fur which happens once or twice a year on average.

Bunnies need a constant supply of fresh, clean drinking water. Generally they will use the animal drinking bottles with the little ball at the end. In winter months it's important that the water be replenished several times a day so it doesn't freeze. Be sure to run hot water over the metal spout with the ball, so it's not frozen and water can actually reach the rabbit. Using a bowl for water during the winter months may prove advantageous, but you might want to get one at a pet supply store with a brace or stand that prevents the rabbit from tipping the bowl over.

Molting

Rabbits will typically molt (shed) their fur, which is a complete shedding of the coat, on average of once or twice a year once they have reached adulthood. This process is fairly intense on a rabbit's health and some extra measures should be given during this time.

It's not uncommon for rabbits to drop weight during a molt. The biggest health risk during a molt is getting hair balls in their intestines from their own grooming. These hair balls can cause deadly blockages in their gut.

When you notice your rabbit starting to shed more than just a few hairs at a time, begin gently brushing him once or twice daily. When it has entered the heavy molt stage, which will be obvious by massive amounts of fur coming out, increase the frequency of brushing, to get as much out, as quickly as possible. A very fine toothed hacksaw blade actually works well during this stage, or any other brush for animals.

It's important to make sure the rabbit is getting plenty of roughage in their diet during this time. Give several handfuls of grass hay daily in addition to its regular food. You can also give it one or two tablets of papaya enzyme as well, or simply a slice of fresh papaya.

You may want to get a hairball supplement from your local vet during this time to assist with prevention.

Something else to feed them during a molt is black oil sunflower seeds (not the common striped variety). These are a good source of fiber, protein, vitamin E, linoleic acid and the extra oil helps pass any fur through their digestive tract. Just add 6 seeds on top of their regular rabbit pellets daily. Don't overdo it.

If you notice the rabbit getting lethargic, just not it's usual perky self, keep a very close eye out. Rabbits tend to go downhill very quickly if something is wrong. If he goes 'off-feed' or anything unusual, like a runny nose, take him to the vet immediately.

Rabbit Tooth Care

Rabbit's teeth continue to grow their entire life. Whether your rabbit is an indoor or outdoor living bunny, make sure it has untreated wood blocks available to chew on. This helps to naturally keep the teeth trimmed down, and it a vital health issue. This is why they have this instinct to chew.

Proper tooth alignment should not be top and bottom teeth meeting in the middle. The normal bite of rabbits' teeth is the top incisors should be slightly in front of the lower teeth. When buying a rabbit, you should check that this is normal. If it's not, it will most likely involve taking your rabbit to a vet several times a year to have the veterinary treat the teeth, so the rabbit can eat. Malformed teeth can be fatal as the rabbit ages, if this is not done.

Toenail Care

Rabbits have sharp toenails that will need to be trimmed often with nail clippers or pet nail clippers. It's better to trim small amounts frequently than large amounts infrequently. It may be necessary to trim nails every week or bi-weekly.

At first this may be a two person job. Depending on the rabbit's temperament, one person may cradle bunny in the arms like a baby, while the other trims the nails. Alternatively, the rabbit could be sitting on a table with a thick towel, then gently lift one foot at a time, and gently trim the nails. For the back legs, one person could hold the rabbit on the towel in a sitting type position, while the other trims the back feet nails. The second person is there is help reassure and distract the rabbit, and keep him from running away.

Be sure not to cut into the vein within the nail, which is very painful and will bleed. You can try to hold the paw and nail up to the light first to see where the vein ends. You can very gently press the pad of the foot to help expose the nail visually. This will give you an idea of how much nail to clip, but be conservative and clip less than that.

They will get used to having their nails trimmed, but if you cut into the quick of the nail, they'll remember that pain, and trimming will be a much harder process in the future. So, proceed carefully. You might want to have some Styptic Powder on hand in case you do nick a vein. You would apply some of this powder with a Q-tip to stop the bleeding.

Allowing their nails to get too long not only increases their risk of accidently ripping their nail on something (very painful), but it increases the risk of them getting a condition known as 'sore hocks', which are painful sores on the bottoms of their feet that can be open and infected. So, keep on top of diligent nail trimming. Once you get the hang of it, its really no big deal.

Preparing your Home for your New Pet Rabbit

Although rabbits have not been considered typical pets like cats and dogs for very long, it is possible to make them a part of your family.

If you allow, they can have play time in your home (or an area fenced off with a baby gate) as long as a few precautions are taken. Alternatively, if there is a safe place outdoors (fenced run or similar situation) away from other animals, enclosed and with your supervision, they can also enjoy some play and exercise outdoors.

We'll be taking a look at both indoor and outdoor housing options.

Many people believe that rabbits do not need much attention, but they do. If you are not planning to spend time with your pet and this means at least 2-3 hours or so per day, it might be best to consider another type of pet. Contrary to popular belief, rabbits enjoy the attention that you pay them.

Rabbits do require maintenance, which means they need their own water bottle, a food dish, a litter box (if you choose to litter box train them), a cage, and a comfy place to sleep. The place you provide for your new pet bunny to sleep should be away from drafts and in an area that is not high traffic. This will allow him to retreat to his special spot for resting.

Your new rabbit will need exercise as well. This is why toys are important and interacting with him will help him to get the exercise needed to be happy and healthy. An area such as an enclosed porch, a room in your home, or simply a section that is gated off, is a good place to put toys for the rabbit to play with when he is ready. It also provides space for him to run and jump. Their antics can be hilarious!

Too much commotion can make rabbits nervous and too many people at once (especially in the beginning), increases the risk that your rabbit could be stepped on or otherwise accidently injured. Adult supervision should always be present with young children.

Basic guidelines should be followed when getting your home ready for all pets. Whether it is a bunny, a kitten or a puppy, they are all babies. Like all babies, you have to watch out for anything that they could get hurt by, swallow, chew, or that could pose a danger to them. Safety is an issue no matter what type of pets are in the household.   Electrical wires are especially hazardous concerning rabbits.

Indoor Living for Rabbits

Rabbits can be litter boxed trained. Generally the rabbit will want to urinate in a certain corner of the house or room. At first, set a litter box (without a lid) into the room. If the rabbit uses a different corner, put the litter box in the corner it does use. Rabbits are clean animals and will tend to use the same area over and over.

Training for the rabbit poop (pellets) is a bit more challenging. Some rabbits will go to the litter box for that too (with time), others you'll have to vacuum up after. The one consolation here is that rabbit pellets are not messy, or very smelly. You could also pick them up with a tissue and place them in the litter box so the rabbit gets the idea to be going there.

The biggest issue with indoor rabbits will be the chewing of cords and furniture. Make sure bunny has plenty of non-painted or varnished wood blocks available to chew (don't use cedar however). Get all electrical cords out of the rabbit's reach. Obviously, it can be deadly if he takes a bite. If your rabbit is given free roam of the house at all times, there is a very real risk your furniture could get chewed on, especially wooden legs. Do not blankets or other 'soft' items in the cage, as he will eat those items.

You may want to get a wire indoor cage (be sure to put some wood to chew on for him in the cage). Keep bunny in the cage at night and when nobody's home, allowing him to come out when you are home, or when it's playtime.

Building a Rabbit Hutch

One could either build their own rabbit hutch, or buy a wire cage (or ready made hutch) and secure it up off the ground. Make sure the cage will be big enough for the breed of rabbit you will be getting. Most rabbits are much larger than most people realize.

The considerations for outdoor housing must be these requirements:

1. Off the ground

2. Wire bottom

3. Protected from the sun

4. Placed in a shady area

5. Protection from rain and wind

6. Protected from dogs or other predators

Within the wire bottom of the cage, you will also need to either have a portion of the hutch be wood bottom, or simply place a 2X3 flat piece of plywood inside the cage. The point is to have an area where the rabbit can get off the wire for part of the day. This is important for proper foot care. Be sure to check the bottom of your rabbit's feet periodically to make sure the fur isn't being worn off and sores developing. This is especially true for the large breeds and those with rex fur. If you notice this happening, see a veterinarian.

Do not put blankets or other similar items in a rabbit's cage. It creates hygiene problems and the rabbit will most likely chew it up and can cause intestinal blockage. If you absolutely can't stand a fairly empty cage, then put plenty of grass hay in there.

Be sure the cage is covered (all three sides) for protection from sun, wind, rain and is safe from predators. A rabbit can survive the cold better than heat, but if a rabbit gets wet, it makes it more susceptible to sickness.

Summer heat can be a challenge, especially in high temps. Rabbits need to be kept as cool as possible, ensure their cage is in shade, especially in the heat of the day. When temps hit over 90 degrees, you'll need to be watching your bunny closer. Rabbits cool off by panting, and their ears are a method of cooling down. If you see your rabbit panting, and their ears feel hot, time to intervene. Take a washcloth with cool water (not ice water), and wring the majority of the water out, then moisten their ears with the cool water. This will help drop their body temperature. Do this several times a day during the hottest part of the day.

Another method is to take a cool water humidifier or other misting system and allow a cool mist to run near the rabbit's living quarters. Setting a large block of ice on the ground below the rabbit's cage will also help drop the temp and provide some relief.

If you want to build a rabbit hutch for your new pet, it is possible if you are the least bit handy. Basic rabbit hutches are made using wire and wood and there is no particular shape that is right or wrong. It depends on your preferences and if the hutch is for one rabbit or more (each should have it's own living space). The basic hutch should have enough room for the rabbit to stand up and have space to stretch and move about.

The hutch should be at least four times larger than your rabbit. If he is still a baby, keep his adult size in mind when you are figuring out the dimension. One of the things that rabbit hutches generally have are two sections. This allows the rabbit to have a separate area for sleeping. If the rabbit hutch is going to be outside, it will need to be off the ground and have a roof. The recommended height is 4 feet above the ground.

Gather all the materials that you will need. This will include the following:

- Two large pieces of plywood – The exact measurements will depend on the size of the rabbit hutch being built.

- Wire mesh – Purchase the type made specifically for rabbits. Chicken wire will not work because it is not as strong and it does not keep out predators. The wire should be 14-gauge or 16-gauge galvanized wire and you will need two sizes. The sides and the top should be either 1" x 2" or 1" x 1" and the floor should be 1/2" x 1" because the rabbit will be standing on this wire.

- Drop tray (optional)

- Roofing materials

- Power saw

- Wire cutters

- Metal file

- C-rings

- Latch

Begin by putting together the frame. Using the 1" x 2" wire and the wire cutters, cut six pieces the length that is needed. For example, a typical rabbit hutch may be 24 inches by 48 inches. If this is the case, you will need to cut two pieces at 24" long and four pieces at 48 inches long.

Next cut a piece of the 1/2" x 1" wire to the same length as the longest pieces that were just cut – 48 inches. Attach the two small length pieces of wire using the C-rings to one of the longer pieces of wire. This will be the beginning of the back and the sides of the rabbit hutch. Now attach two of the 48-inch pieces of wire that you cut to the top and the bottom of the pieces you just put together. Use the C-rings to do this as well. Make sure you are using the 1/2" wire for the bottom, but attach it several inches above the actual bottom to leave room for the drop tray (or you can allow droppings to fall to the ground).

Attach another piece of wire with the C-rings to form the front of the cage. A divider should be cut from the plywood. Cut holes in the edges and a hole in one end, large enough for the rabbit to go through. Next attach this to the wire on the inside of the cage, about halfway or at 24 inches using the C-rings. Attach it to the front and the back. Place the top on the cage and attach it to the sides with C-rings and to the top of the divider.

The last piece of wire can be attached to the bottom of the cage. This will be for sliding the drop tray in and out and it will hold it in place as well. Using the wire cutters, make an opening on the front of the cage for sliding the drop tray in and out as needed. Now make a place for the door. At the front of the cage, cut an opening. The rough edges can be covered with trim eliminating the

sharp edges. Using leftover wire, cut a piece that is a bit

larger than the opening you just cut. Take this piece and

attach it to the left side of the opening using the C-rings.

Put a latch on the other side to keep the hutch securely

closed when needed.

Now it is time to make the frame for your rabbit hutch.

Using 2" x 4" lumber, cut it to lengths that are just a bit

bigger than the cage you have just built. Put the pieces

together, making certain that the cage fits inside. Next

cut pieces of the 2" x 4" lumber for the legs. They should

be four feet long. Attach the legs to the bottom of the

frame just built with nails. They need to be securely

attached, so the frame does not wobble. The cage should

slide easily into the frame.

For added strength, you can cut pieces of plywood the same dimensions as the front, back and sides of the frame and attach them permanently. They can also be attached with hinges so they can be opened. This will allow more air into the rabbit hutch. The roof can be built now. Cut a piece of plywood that totally covers the top of the rabbit hutch. Nail the plywood to the top of the frame, making certain it is secure. If you want you can add plastic, metal or shingles to the top of this plywood to provide added protection for the rabbits.

Tips for the Prospective Rabbit Owner

If you are ready to find the right breed of rabbit for a pet, there are a number of places that you can try. Breeders can guide you in the right direction to find one that is of a good temperament for a pet. As mentioned previously at the beginning there are different breeds available and some are more suited for pets than others. Owning a pet rabbit can be both rewarding as well as a learning experience.

Rabbits can offer kids a terrific way to participate in 4-H. They will learn many lessons from caring for the rabbits, to handling and showing them. This is also a great assignment for learning responsibility. Those who participate in a 4-H pet rabbit project will learn many skills, including the opportunity to help pass their knowledge along to others, and to become a leader.

Hopefully they will make some positive, lifelong friends along the way.

If you have a pet rabbit that is aggressive and mean, here are some tips to hopefully turn the situation around. First off, I recommend allowing a patient adult to take over sole care of the rabbit. A couple reasons for this, is you don't want children to get attacked or bit, and you are tying to re-habilitate the rabbit socially. That will become easier when only one person is dealing with the rabbit.

First off, access the living situation. Is there another rabbit living in the same cage, or nearby? Isolate the mean one and have it live elsewhere, completely far away from the other. I have had a couple of mean ones over the years (a very trying situation) and in nearly every case, it came down to a female, who was dealing with reproductive cycles due to being in proximity to males and other rabbits. There are simply some who get aggressive in that environment and become extra territorial as well. This type of rabbit should be in a single rabbit type situation.

Secondly, avoid putting your hand in their cage. Not that you will want to, but sometimes you might have to. Find another way. Putting your hand in their cage, kicks in the territorial fight aspect, your hand is in their turf. Use a water and feeding system that doesn't require your hand inside.

Daily, try to coax the rabbit out of the cage for playtime. If housed outdoors, maybe that means putting a long wooden board from the open door to a gated area on the ground, so it can walk down the board to the ground. Leave it alone until it gets on the ground on its own.

Once there, get in the area with the rabbit and try to offer it treats, like an apple slice. Allow it to hop around as you sit with it. Gradually, try to pet the rabbit. These same principals apply if the rabbit lives indoors. Try to make this a good experience.

With time and patience, many will turn around and be fine. They may never become the friendliest on the block, they might never be ones you reach a hand in their cage, and they might not ever be suitable pets for children. But the can become enjoyable, peaceable companions for adults.

In every case that I had a mean rabbit, all of them eventually came out of it and was fine, although I was always cautious with them. It is worth the effort.

I hope you have found value in this book and that you enjoy the amazing world of pet rabbits!

By Amber Richards

Please drop by Amber's website at: Books by Amber Richards

If you enjoyed this book or received value from it in any way, would you be kind enough to leave a review for this book on Amazon? I would be so grateful. Thank you!

Printed in Great
Britain
by Amazon